LET GOOD FORTUNE JUMP ON YOU

LET GOOD FORTUNE JUMP ON YOU

Good Karma Publishing

Fort Yates 1990

Reprint of 1986 Eldorado Mountain Yoga Ashram edition

GOOD KARMA PUBLISHING, INC., Publisher
Box 511
Fort Yates, ND 58538

Printed in the United States of America by BookMasters, Inc., Ashland, OH

First Good Karma Publishing, Inc. edition: 1990

Words and brushwork by Paul Reps
Layout by Jean Katus
♲ *Text printed on recycled paper*

Library of Congress Catalog Card Number 90-82900

ISBN 0-9620812-7-2

FOREWORD

I first met Paul Reps in Los Angeles in 1954. We immediately decided to lunch together. On the way to the coffee shop, we passed a toy store that had a chess set in the window. Reps asked me if I played the game, and when I answered in the affirmative, we crawled into the window and played a while.

After lunch we stood in line to pay our checks. Arriving at the counter and noticing the harassed look on the cashier's face, Reps commented to her: "I bet you have a lovely smile!" She instantly brightened. Someone was paying attention to her!

A postcard from Reps found me in India. It said, "India is full of Saints and Aints," the inference being that there were more Aints than Saints. Later he wrote: "India is a terrible place, let's face it. In order to do that, we have to have a face."

When my original publisher, Sun Books, and I agreed that there should be a book of Reps' cards, letters, and drawings mailed to me over the years, Reps wrote me saying sternly that there must be no reference to sex or the stock market. I wrote back that we were not doing a book called *Saint Reps.* (It was rumored that Reps had children in New Zealand, Sweden, and possibly elsewhere.) He was always successful in the market, mostly on an intuitive basis, although he was a good stock market chartist as well.

Though Reps studied Zen and was close to Zen figures and though he became immersed in Sufism after being with the great teacher, Inayat Khan, for a time (he then began using the name "Saladin Reps"), he was a unique man and followed his own way, the "Path of Joy," as he explained it to me.

I could tell innumerable amusing stories about this remarkable person who just passed away at age 94, but anyone reading *Zen Flesh, Zen Bones;* *Zen Telegrams;* or this book will see the man reflected in his writing.

All over the world Saints, Sages, and Aints know Reps well. He is highly thought of in Japan, where his picture poems were made into Obis (thick sashes, sometimes highly decorated, tied around the waist of the kimono)! Since Reps' recent passing, a legend is sure to arise around the world.

Reps was a timeless man who never owned a telephone. "Phone me in the rice fields," he would say. Those who did have had their lives enriched.

Justin F. Stone
July 1990

INTRODUCTION

Paul Reps has spent most of his ninety years wandering the globe, finding the humor and surprise in life. His travels began in 1915 when a white-haired librarian introduced him to the *Bhagavad Gita* and the *Upanishads*. Several weeks later, Reps was working his passage to India as a crew member on a ship. He "went deep into the Himalayas, where the tigers roared every night, and began to live as they lived there." His travels include ten years in Japan, as well as visits to Asia, Europe and beyond.

Reps expresses his unique perspective of man and world through dozens of books, essays, and newspaper articles published throughout the world. His most famous book is *Zen Flesh, Zen Bones*. At the urging of the head of a large Zen monastery, Reps began to combine simple poems with his own style of Japanese Sumi-e painting. He calls them "picture poems." The drawings are intentionally crude or as Reps says, "primal." To the inattentive eye they may say little, but when pondered in a Zen kind of way they offer the explosive insight of a lifetime.

Faith Stone
1986

ask

the

grassblades

neps

WHEN WE BLINK
WE ANTI-THINK

WHEN WE LISTEN
WE GLISTEN

WHEN WE FEEL
WE REAL

now

STand
STAMP
Feet

BLINK

early mornings south american indians
sit and blink into sunlight
as an inner opening practice
letting inlight through
have you some indian blood too?

NOT BODY
NOT MIND
WHO AM I?

sign here

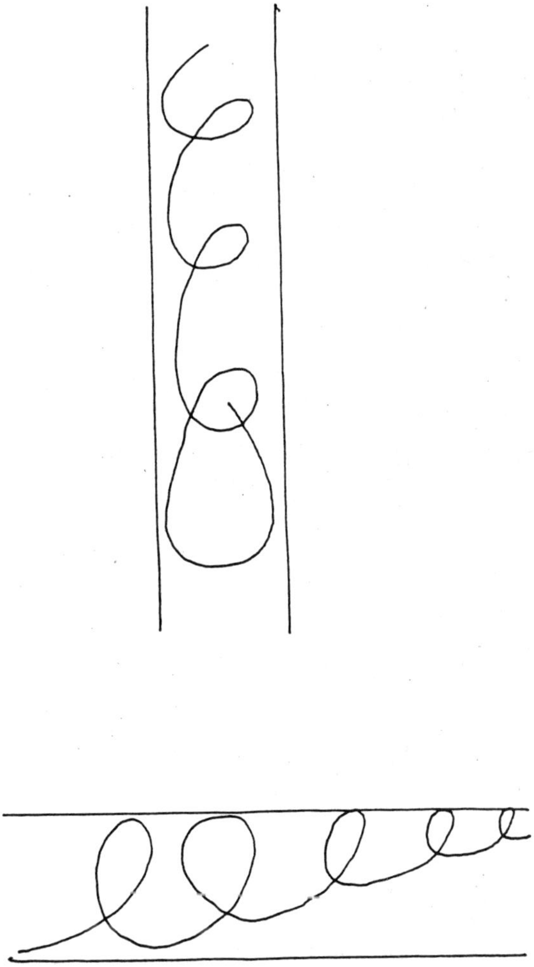

springing

one blink
self-erasing

makes way
for another blink

in our imaging/imagining

"so what seems true?"

N O T H I N G N E S S

wherefrom arises
SOMETHINGNESS
MADE OF DESIRES
and
THESE VANISHING
IN DEEP SLEEP
and in
DEEP WAKING
"well, I don't want
to vanish"
WHO WANTS WHAT
YOU ARE ALREADY
99/100ths
IN-VISIBLE

p a u s e

We often p a u s e
before expressing
something

May we find this pre-act
freshing healing too

To win the life game
when breathflow pauses out
keep out

when breathflow pauses in
keep in

feel

one

feel one
experience
many

"how do I
feel one?"

naturally

these
pages
declare
you

free

and

freeing

but you need not be / you are welcome to be hooked with words / kith, kin, father, mother, friend, politician, doctor, preacher, scientist, lover primal

hungry

social

jabber

100 mountain
climbers
sleep same room
no two
same dream

no two snowflakes same
each exquisitely designed
- a disregarded
scientific fact

our cells
cellebrating
l i g h t

laugh l i g h t

so
its
all
right

WE

MEET

A

CHILD

child at once

feels "are you

aliving?

do you feel play

as I do?"

HOW DO WE NOT LOSE OUR PLAY WAY? ? ?

A

SEE AND SAY

ARE NOT THE WAY

B

YOU ARE THE WAY

C

OH !

A LIGHT WAVE

join
us

Bob: "It works"

Ralph: "Simple
magic"

Mary: "Makes men
bearable"

Dorothy:
"My trouble melts
away"

Jack: "Has me in
control"

Edith: "We do it with
another -
We do not think
(separatively)
We let it happen"

Gene: "Just sit"

Ruth: "Why so beneficial?
Because we see it
this way?"

enter
the
dear
silencing

Ann: "Who, me?"

my child

naturally a woman
wants to have a child

child grows and runs away
taken from her
"How did it happen?"

It happens with the verb
'have'

my child

when saying
we make a noise
love you

a male attracted to
a female

the female
attracted to the male
thinks "would he be
a good father for
my child"

her thought veers
to child

the male perhaps
attracted to
another female

is bird-love like this?

w h e n s e n s i n g s subside
wave re-turns to sea

touch

TOUCH FACE

HEART AREA

"why?"

graduating from possessive
habiting "my child"

"how do we do that?"

TOUCHING

no
body
owns
another
body

no
mind
owns
another
mind

we overeagerly TIGHTEN
HERE AND THERE
THROUGH OUR NERVE/MUSCLE SYSTEM

AND
LEAVE
IT
TIGHT

AND
MOVE
AGAINST US

SO
WE
ARE
AGAINST
US

LET'S
BLOW
OUR
TIGHT
AWAY

"you're telling me I can be as flexive as cat
simply by blowing my TIGHT away?"

YES

"O K I'm blowing"

"where do I blow next?"

"it feels loose and free"

head rolling

soft eyes closed
let head roll around
in a slowing circle
up right side with
 inbreathflow
down left with
 outbreathflow

softens nerves in neck
and back, restores
natural breath-rhythm

if you suffer
an ache or pain or stiffness
somewhere in you

or if you just suffer

do this:

CRAWL AROUND
TO A GOOD PLACE
(the crawl helps too)

ON BACK

PUSH RIGHT HEEL FAR DOWN
PUSH LEFT HEEL FAR DOWN
THEN
PULL BOTH KNEES UP TIGHT TO CHEST
AND SQUEEZE THEM HERE
AND
SLOWLY S L O W L Y
SWING HELD KNEES TO RIGHT
THEN FAR TO LEFT
NERVE/MUSCLES OF ENTIRE BACK
P R E S S
S Q U E E Z E
L O O S E N
HOW GOOD IT FEELS

THIS BOOK GIVES SOMETHINGS
TO DO
ALREADY DOING TO HAVE YOU
AS NEW ALL THROUGH

a kind of inner life education

Sniff

STAND
FEET PARALLEL
FOR INTEGRITY
SHAKE LEFT HAND OFF
SHAKE RIGHT HAND OFF
SHAKE BOTH HANDS OFF

LIGHT STRAIGHT ARMS
CLOSE TO EARS
HIGHER

INTERMESH FINGERS OF HANDS
BEHIND BACK
DRAWING CLASPED HANDS
HIGHER

internal organs
up and back
into place

prey

SPEAKING or SINGING
releases ENERGY
with outbreathflow

With inbreathflow
r e c e i v e

L I G H T (ENERGY)

FLOWS INTO
SOUND (soul)

FREEZES (into
form)

ALLAH
GOD
DEITY
ENERGY

Moslems and Christians
fight over names for 1,000 years

"How does a word
pop into my head?"

YOU LET IT

"how do I let it?"

YOU IN-VITE IT IN

"what goes on
before I let it?"

YOU ARE FREE (OF
WORDS)

"what does this free
do for me?"

IT ENERGISES
AS IN
DEEP SLEEP
WITHOUT WORDS

ENERGISING

in

joy.

w i t h o u t

p l a y

we lose

our way

any slight motion surprise = p l a y

without light
we would not be

suppose there are
other suns

suppose

tasting
light
evering

suppose
bliss this

---

your photo here

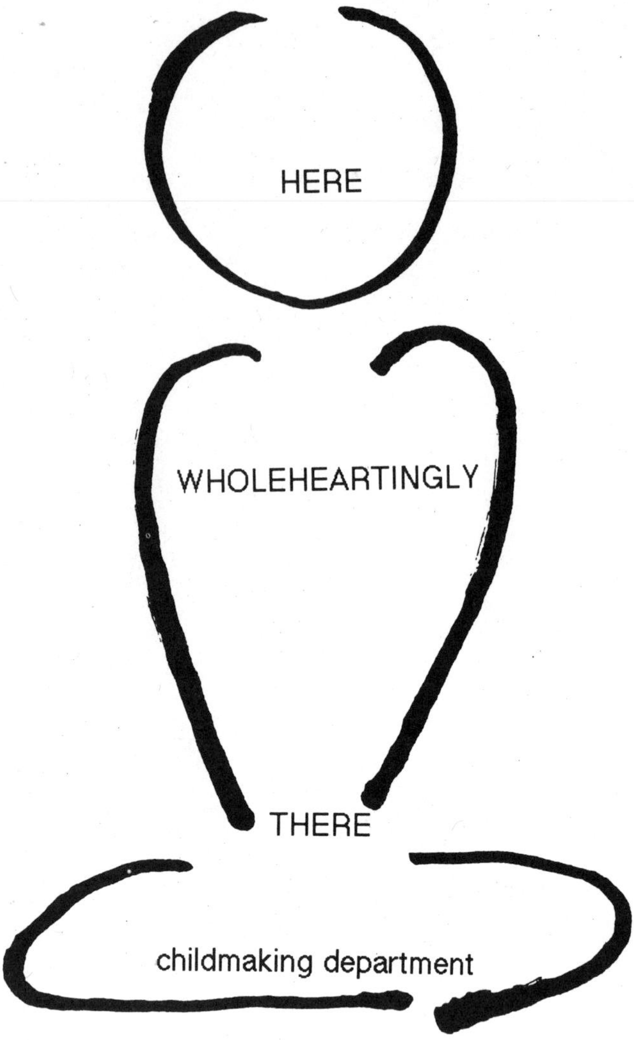
HERE
WHOLEHEARTINGLY
THERE
childmaking department

heartflow
breathflow

me

I don't know

what you will say next

you don't know what -
I will say NEXT

surprise!

3 times out of 4
w r o n g

OUTDOORS
FORGIVES

the instant we step outdoors
L I G H T fills air caresses

some slightest motion
as
lifting finger
gently head turning

INDOORS

LIGHT our father-mother
AIR our first food
sister brother

only
be-ing

RESTING ON BACK

WITH LEGS UP ON CHAIR OR BED

"Why? Aren't there more urgent
things to do?"

BLOODFLOW

FREELY FLOWING

TURNS ON

\ /
GENIUS
/ \

suddenly

free

of

"me"

from here . . to there

ask WHO . . walks 

ask WHO . . walks 

probably each child asks
this question
W H O
W O N D E R O U S L Y

not only are we
in touch with
each human of our world
with or without telephone
we are in touch with
their warm love
and
adoration
as they are
with ours

how to
enter
ever,

OPENING

ARMS

TO SKY

WITH INBREATHFLOW

RECEIVING

LIGHTLY

lower arms

"Why ache, why pain?"

NO SLOW MOTION

LET HEAD TURN
SLOWLY
S L O W L Y

s l o w

m o t i o n

c
o
R
E
S

c o m m o t i o n

each

feast

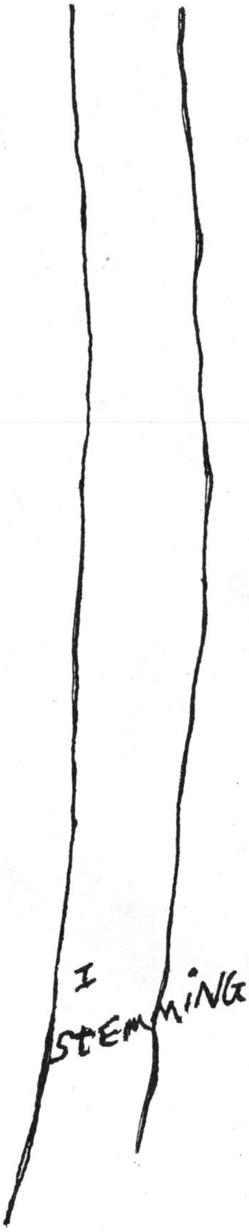

bundles of words
we name mind

OUR VERY SELF

WE EXPERIENCE
SILENTLY

BE-ING

FREE AND
FREEING

LET US ASSUME
YOU AS ALIVE

THIS MEANS YOU ARE
WITH NATURAL BREATHFLOW

outbreathflow

inbreathflow

16 times each minute
for an hour 16 x 60 = 960 times

WHAT ARE YOU DOING 960 TIMES EACH DAY?
ANSWER: nothing

since you are not breathing
but are being breathed

HOW THANKFULL WE MIGHT BE

are we?

picture-writing. lines freeze sound. shapes surface INlight black water brushed flows from heart. your line sings you

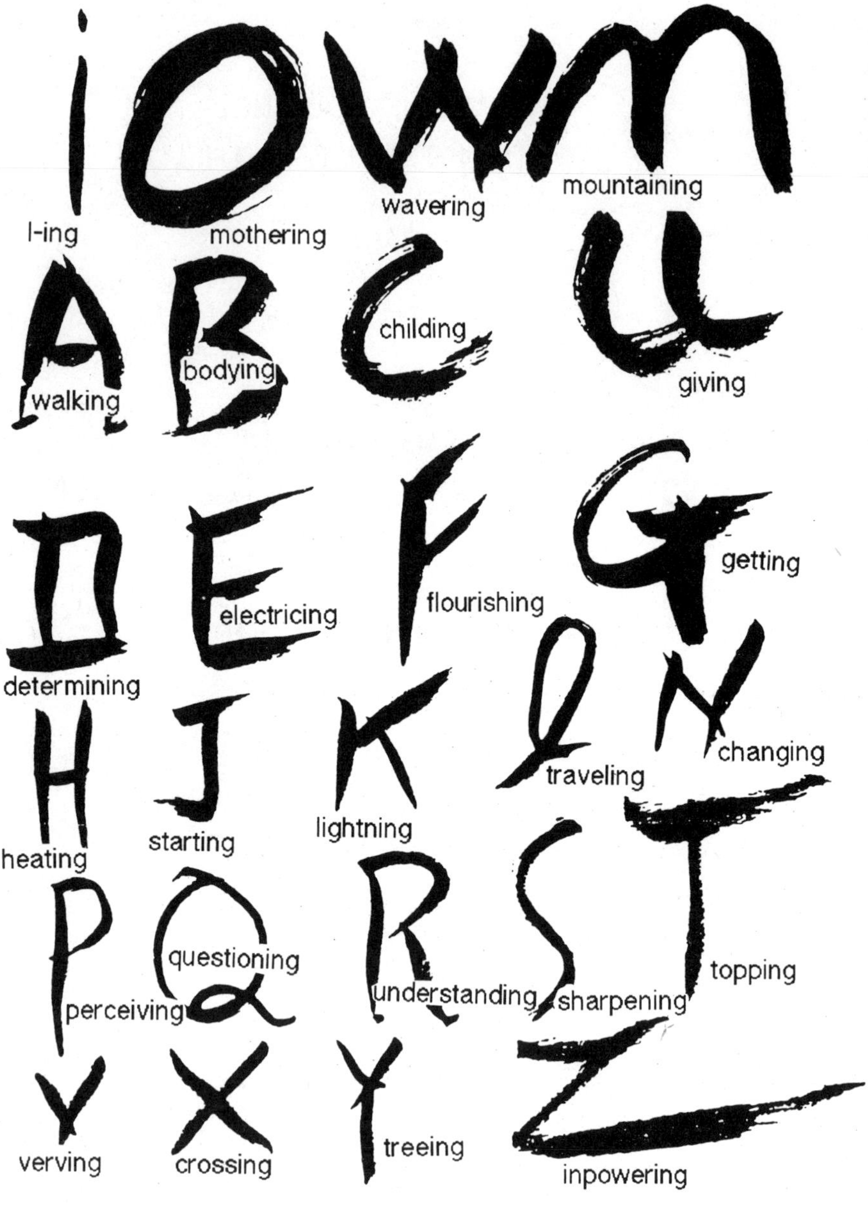

Make a deck of cards with a letter on each card / ASK A QUESTION / Shuffle and draw a card / Dare you intuit you ??

birds
free
why not
we

running

backward

into

light

CAN YOU COUNT TO 3 ?

1

2

3

“we project numbers and
letters but how do we
get back into real me?”

3

2

1

unitive experiencing
transforming me-ing
into be-ing

O

SILENT TONING

HUMMMMMM

MMMMMMMM

FEEL GOOD

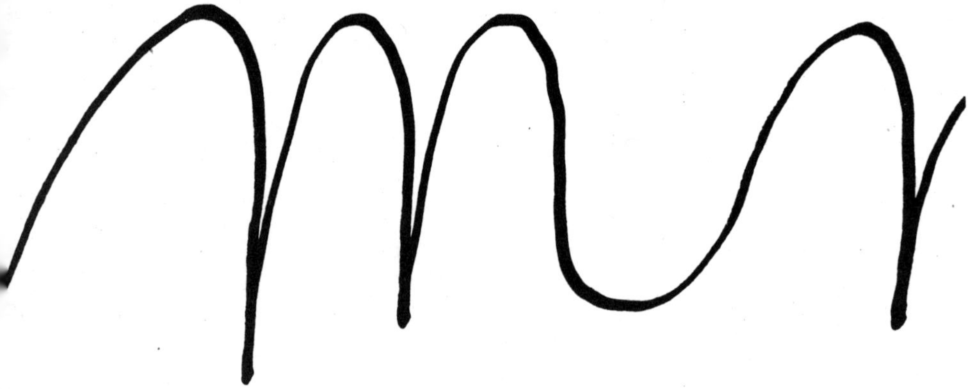

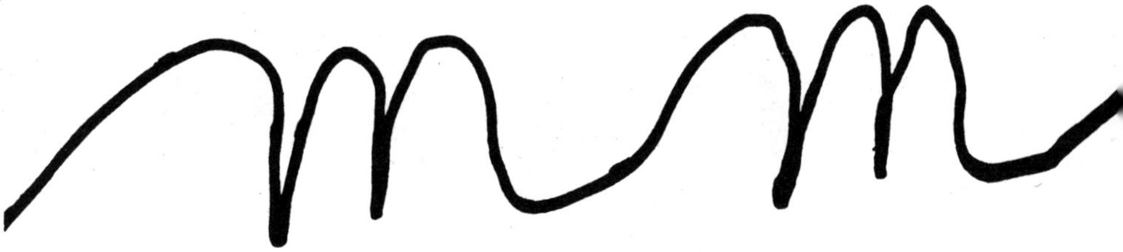

In old fruit-abundant hawaii
the child received with open love and joy
each child with multiple parents
possessiveness unknown

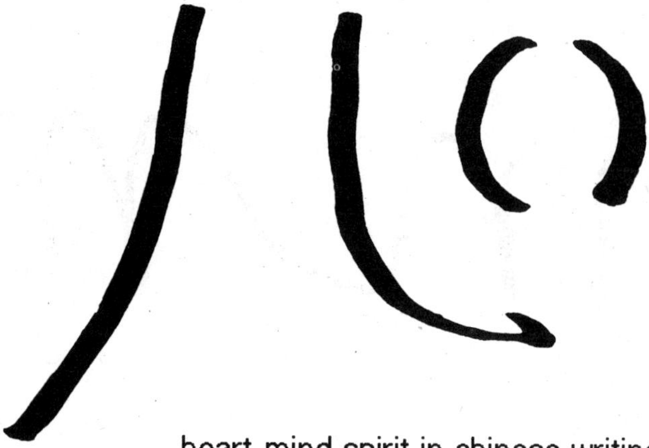

heart mind spirit in chinese writing
one   -inbreathflow worth

*a
thousand
sighs*

do we turn on our

INLIGHT

as we turn on a

LIGHT

SUPPOSE
WE LIGHT A CANDLE
OR A SMALL STICK OF INCENSE
DEDICATING
THIS LIGHT TO THE
INLIGHT OF YOU

an oriental custom of respect

bLUE

GReen

given us

some humans find
when dying:
"OH IT'S ALL LIGHT!"

so why not live
in L I G H T?

"how do I do that?"

(WE ALREADY LIVE
IN L I G H T)

if you disagree and feel that we don't
live in light at all,
then you live in darkness?

If you agree and radiate l i g h t, does
everyone love you ?

drawing

come into

the dear s i l e n c i n g

of the artist

the scientist

originator

child

this 4-way picture
by meghan, age 2

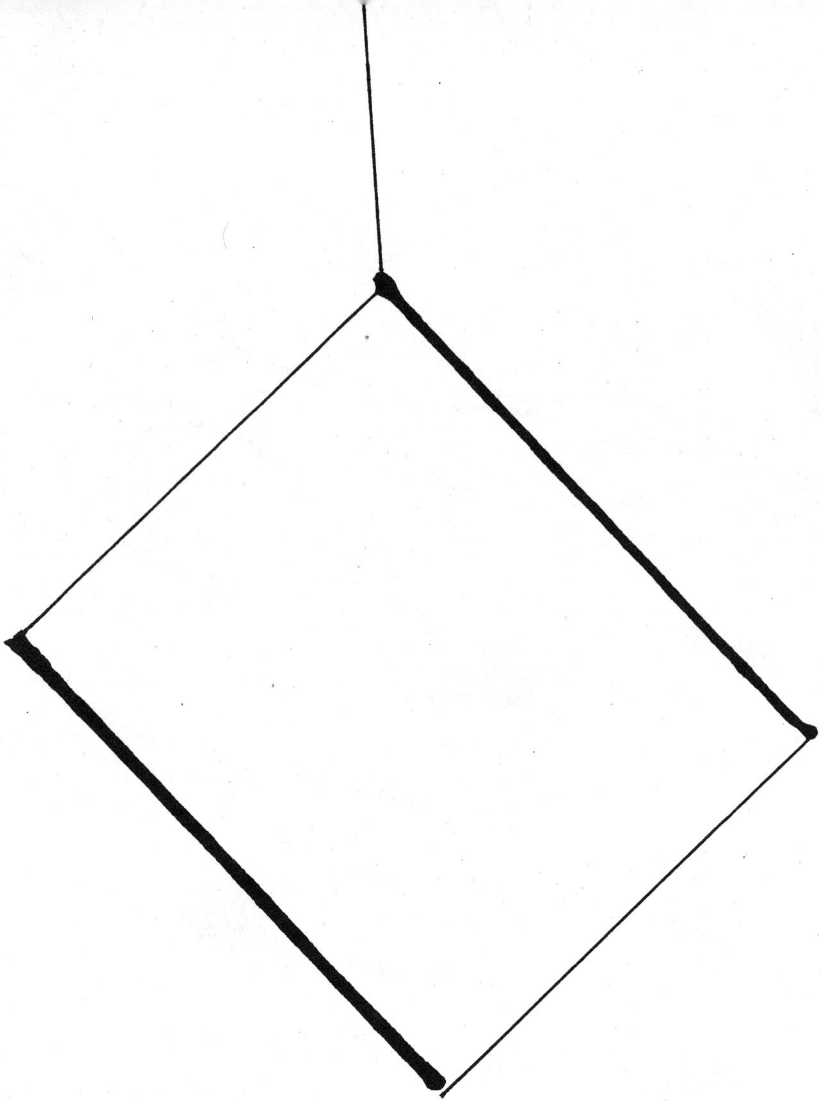

RECTANGULARISM
explained

no rectangular shape
found in
great nature

humans invent such
shape for building
caves without light
from above

then spend much time
in them, often
multi-storied

RECTANGULARISM
exposed

HANG A RECTANGULAR
ALL-GOLD CARDBOARD
ON A THREAD

see it silently
mind-move with
wind

RECTANGULARISM CURED

step outdoors!

"how can I be
considered
cured if I
step indoors
again?"

then step indoors again
only it isn't 'again'

but FRESH FRESH FRESH

CURE FOUND

IN SPRING STEP OUTDOORS

EACH STEP A SPRING

FULL OF SPRINGS OF JOY

STEPPING INTO

THE ALL SELF

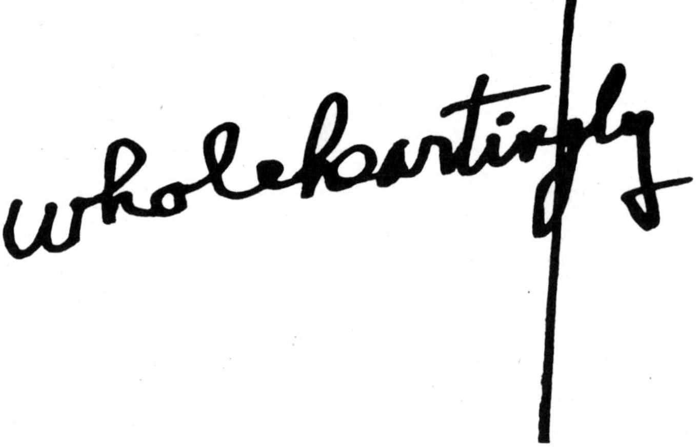

stretch
breath flow

HOW TO SAY

YES

How to
SAY

No

do this:

lips closed
swallow air

back and up

high higher
opening inner
a w a r e

and

a silent sound as HAAAAA
on natural outbreathflow

and SAAAAA with inbreathflow

HAAAAA (out) SAAAAA (in)

(you are already doing this
21,000 times daily)
as breathflow flows freeing

(
inner

be-ing

let

good fortune

jump

on

you

leaps

COLOPHON

The body type chosen for this book is Helvetica and Helvetica Bold for the headlines. The text paper is 60-pound white recycled. The cover is 12-point CIS with lamination. One thousand copies comprised the first Good Karma Publishing printing completed in the fall of 1990.